SPOT 50
Seashore

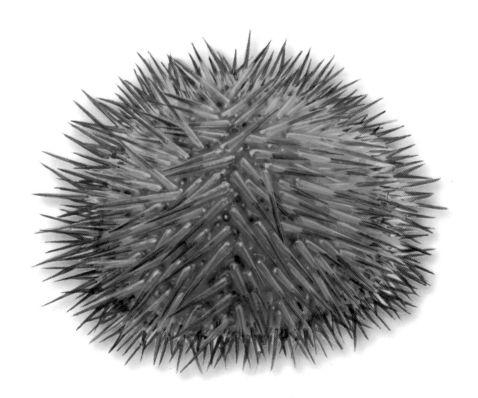

Camilla de la Bedoyere

Miles Kelly

First published in 2012 by Miles Kelly Publishing Ltd
Harding's Barn, Bardfield End Green, Thaxted, Essex, CM6 3PX, UK

Copyright © Miles Kelly Publishing Ltd 2012

This edition printed in 2013

2 4 6 8 10 9 7 5 3 1

Publishing Director Belinda Gallagher
Creative Director Jo Cowan
Editor Claire Philip
Designers Jo Cowan, Kayleigh Allen
Production Manager Elizabeth Collins
Reprographics Stephan Davis, Thom Allaway

ISBN 978-1-84810-906-3

Printed in China

British Library Cataloguing-in-Publication Data
A catalogue record for this book is available from the British Library

ACKNOWLEDGEMENTS
The publishers would like to thank Alan Harris, Bridgette James, Andrea Morandi
and Mike Saunders, who contributed artwork used in this book

The publishers would also like to thank the following sources for the use of their photographs:
Cathy Miles 4(cl)
Shutterstock.com 4(tl) Sarah Pettegree, (cr) godrick,
(bl) Brian Maudsley, (br) David Hughes

All other images are from the Miles Kelly Archives

Made with paper from a sustainable forest

www.mileskelly.net
info@mileskelly.net

www.factsforprojects.com

CONTENTS

Seashore habitats 4
Coastal species 5

🐟 FISH
○ Basking shark 6
○ Lesser sand eel 7
○ Lesser weever fish 8
○ Rock goby 9
○ Shanny 10

🌿 SEAWEED
○ Bladder wrack 11
○ Dulse 12
○ Knotted wrack 13
○ Oarweed 14
○ Sea lettuce 15

⭐ STARFISH, URCHINS & ANEMONES
○ Beadlet anemone 16
○ Brittlestar 17
○ Edible sea urchin 18
○ Green sea urchin 19
○ Starfish 20

🐚 MOLLUSCS
○ Common cockle 21
○ Common limpet 22
○ Common mussel 23
○ Common periwinkle 24
○ Dog whelk 25
○ Painted topshell 26
○ Razor clam 27

PLANTS
○ Glasswort 28
○ Marram grass 29

○ Scarlet pimpernel 30
○ Sea kale 31
○ Sea pea 32
○ Silverweed 33
○ Thrift 34

CRUSTACEANS
○ Hermit crab 35
○ Northern acorn barnacle 36
○ Sand hopper 37
○ Shore crab 38
○ Shrimp 39
○ Velvet swimming crab 40

INSECTS
○ Cinnabar moth 41
○ Common blue butterfly 42
○ Grayling butterfly 43
○ Green tiger beetle 44
○ Red-banded sand wasp 45

BIRDS
○ Avocet 46
○ Common tern 47
○ Cormorant 48
○ Curlew 49
○ Herring gull 50
○ Knot 51
○ Oystercatcher 52
○ Redshank 53
○ Ringed plover 54
○ Shelduck 55

Glossary 56

Tick the circles when you have spotted the species.

SEASHORE HABITATS

A seashore is a place where the sea or ocean meets the land. There are lots of different types of seashore, but they are all exciting habitats where many animal and plant species live.

Saltmarshes
Sea water may cover parts of a saltmarsh every day, or just occasionally. Wading birds and wildfowl feed and breed in these habitats.

Estuaries, mud and sand flats
When the tide goes out, mud and sand deposits are often left behind to create areas of sediment called flats. Estuaries are formed where rivers meet the sea.

Rocky shores and rock pools
When the tide goes out rock pools are great places to find wildlife. The best ones to investigate are the ones closest to the sea.

Sandy beaches and the strandline
These habitats are always changing, as wind and water continually shift the sand. Strandlines are the highest places the sea reaches on a beach.

Shingle beaches
Covered in multi-coloured pebbles, shingle beaches are tough places to live and grow. Some plants, such as sea lavender, are hardy enough to survive.

Sand dunes
Dunes develop when the wind moves sand to a place where it can collect and build up. They often change and move as the wind moves dry sand easily.

COASTAL SPECIES

You'll be amazed at the incredible range of coastal wildlife to be found on British shores. From seaweed to sharks, there is always something fascinating to spot – this guide includes some of the many different animal and plant types you can discover.

		DESCRIPTION
	FISH	Most seashore fish are found in rock pools or shallow water – except for the basking shark, which can be spotted from some coasts.
	SEAWEEDS	Plant-like seaweeds lie exposed on beaches and rocks at low tide, but they sway with the waves when emersed underwater.
	STARFISH, URCHINS & ANEMONES	These unusual-looking sea creatures are commonly found in rock pools and on rocky shores. Starfish and anemones hunt live prey, while urchins eat mostly algae.
	MOLLUSCS	These shelled animals are commonly found on our seashores. Look out for their empty shells dotted along the strandline after high tide.
	PLANTS	Coastal plants are hardy enough to survive the changing weather conditions, often living in salty water or in exposed environments.
	CRUSTACEANS	Crabs, shrimp, barnacles and other members of this group have a hard outer-body casing, segmented bodies and antennae.
	INSECTS	Insects such as the green tiger beetle and red-banded sand wasp buzz, crawl and fly in coastal areas.
	BIRDS	Seashores are great places to find food – and so birds flock to wade, swim and soar around coastal habitats.

Seashore safety

Coasts are brilliant places to discover wildlife, but they can be dangerous – always be prepared by:

- Having an adult nearby when you are exploring seashores.
- Finding out when high and low tide will be, so you don't get stranded.
- Staying away from cliff edges, soft mud and large waves (especially at rocky coasts).
- Checking the weather forecast – make sure you are dressed for the conditions, especially if it is warm, cold or windy.

Scale diagrams

To help you identify your seashore finds, they are shown to scale in relation to an average adult's hand or height.

180 cm

18 cm

BASKING SHARK

Among the world's largest fish, basking sharks are harmless to humans. They swim with their huge mouths agape and filter very small animals from the water. They do not actively prey on other animals. Unlike most fish, basking sharks do not lay eggs. Instead, they give birth to several live young that can each measure up to 2 metres long.

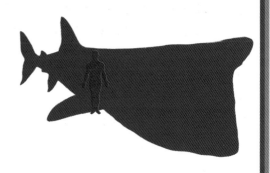

SCALE

Basking sharks are slow swimmers but they can breach — jump out of the water. No one knows why they do this.

FACT FILE

Scientific name
Cetorhinus maximus

Type Cartilaginous fish

Size Up to 10 m

Habitat Open oceans and some coasts

Other names None

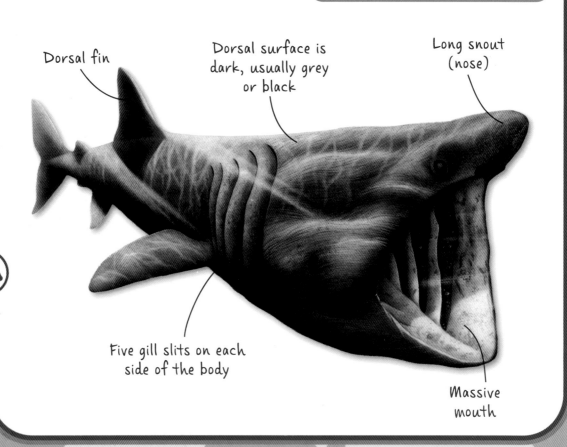

Dorsal fin

Dorsal surface is dark, usually grey or black

Long snout (nose)

Five gill slits on each side of the body

Massive mouth

LESSER SAND EEL

Shoals of these little silvery fish dart **through shallow water in coastal areas, but dive into the sand at any sign of danger.** Lesser sand eels are common in many coastal areas in the summertime but they spend the cool winter months buried deep in the sand. They have reflective scales, which give them a shimmering appearance, but the scales on their backs are actually yellow-green.

SCALE

FACT FILE

Scientific name
Ammodytes tobianus

Type Bony fish

Size Up to 20 cm

Habitat Shallow water, and to depths of 30 m

Other names Sand lance

Lesser sand eels breed in spring and autumn and each female can lay up to 40,000 eggs

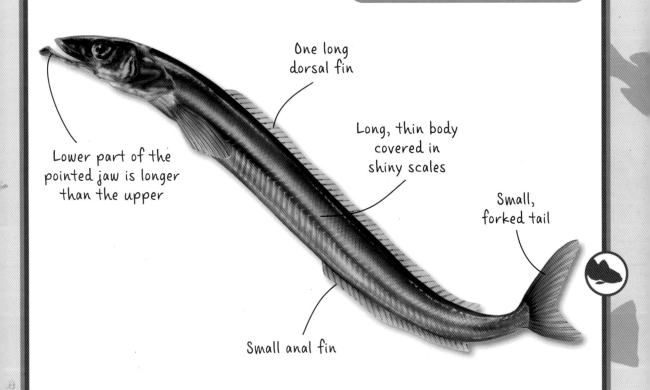

One long dorsal fin

Long, thin body covered in shiny scales

Lower part of the pointed jaw is longer than the upper

Small, forked tail

Small anal fin

LESSER WEEVER FISH

Unsuspecting swimmers and fishermen are **occasionally stung by weever fish.** They are equipped with venomous spines on their backs, which they use for defence. Handling, or standing on, a weever fish can result in a very painful sting. These animals lurk on the sandy sea floor, waiting for smaller fish to pass by. They then leap forwards, grabbing their prey in their large mouths using vicious-looking teeth.

SCALE

FACT FILE

Scientific name
Echiichthys vipera

Type Bony fish

Size Up to 15 cm

Habitat Sandy shores, and in deep water

Other names Weever fish

Weever fish are poor swimmers and can scarcely manage 50 cm before falling to the seafloor.

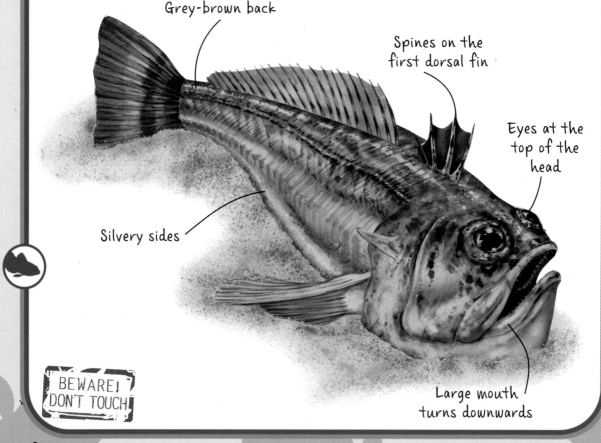

Grey-brown back

Spines on the first dorsal fin

Eyes at the top of the head

Silvery sides

Large mouth turns downwards

BEWARE! DON'T TOUCH

ROCK GOBY

These sturdy little fish are distinctive, with their rounded heads and large, frilled fins. Rock gobies are common around rocky shores, and can be spotted in seaweed, under stones and in rock pools. The fins on their undersides are fused together to create a sucker that sticks to rocks, and stops the fish from being pushed and pulled around by waves. Rock gobies feed on worms, crustaceans and small fish.

SCALE

Male gobies look after the eggs. They turn black when they do this important job.

FACT FILE

Scientific name
Gobius paganellus

Type Bony fish

Size Up to 12 cm

Habitat Rocky shores to depths of 15 m

Other names None

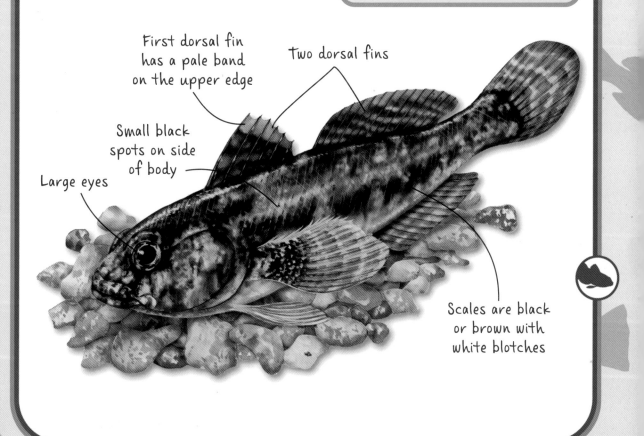

First dorsal fin has a pale band on the upper edge

Two dorsal fins

Small black spots on side of body

Large eyes

Scales are black or brown with white blotches

SHANNY

Although shannies are common, especially in rock pools, they can be hard to spot. These fish are very well camouflaged. Their slimy skin is coloured in a range of olive-brown and dark blotches to help hide them among seaweed, mud and stones. Shannies eat a varied diet and can devour seaweed, as wells as barnacles and other small coastal creatures. In the winter, they move out of rock pools and into shallow waters to avoid the worst effects of winter storms.

SCALE

Shannies can use their strong fins to crawl under stones and disappear from view when hungry birds are around.

FACT FILE

Scientific name
Lipophrys pholis
Type Bony fish
Size Up to 16 cm
Habitat Rock pools, beds of seaweed and stony shores
Other names Common blenny

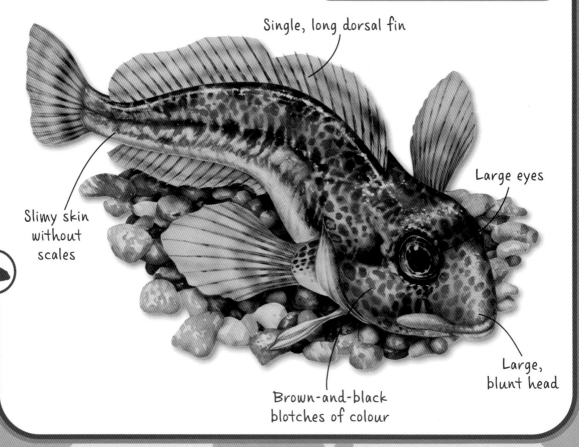

Single, long dorsal fin

Large eyes

Slimy skin without scales

Large, blunt head

Brown-and-black blotches of colour

BLADDER WRACK

This seaweed is common on rocky shores and is easy to identify. When the tide goes out, slippery strands of bladder wrack stretch out over stones and pebbles. The fronds are covered in pairs of round air bladders, which help them to float. This allows the seaweed to reach the sunlight and grow, but the air bladders may be absent if exposed to large waves.

SCALE

The tips of the fronds of bladder wrack are often paler in colour, and covered with round, swollen areas. These are used in reproduction.

FACT FILE

Scientific name
Fucus vesiculosus

Type Brown algae

Size 50–200 cm

Habitat Rocky shores especially on the middle-shore, estuaries

Other name Rock wrack

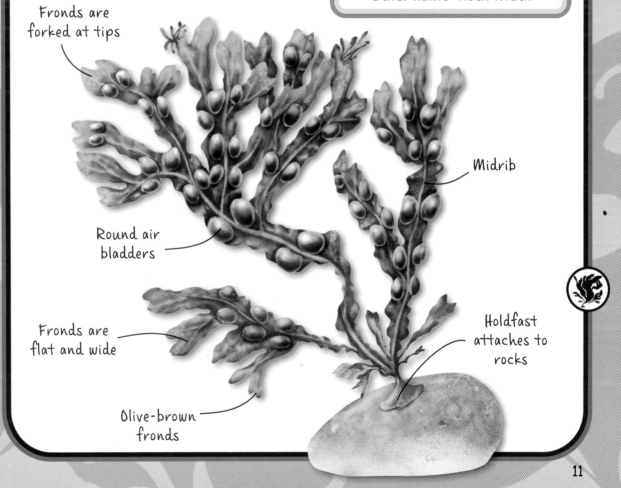

Fronds are forked at tips

Midrib

Round air bladders

Fronds are flat and wide

Holdfast attaches to rocks

Olive-brown fronds

DULSE

This commonly found seaweed can be used as food. Its long, leathery fronds can grow quite wide and become tougher as they age. The ends of the fronds are divided into flat lobes and are usually paler than the rest of the alga. Dulse can be found on rocky shores at low tide and in shallow waters. Long, narrow lobes indicate that the seaweed has been exposed to strong waves.

SCALE

FACT FILE

Scientific name
Palmaria palmata

Type Red algae

Size 20–50 cm

Habitat Lower shore, especially rocky shores

Other name Dilsk

Dulse is often eaten dried or fresh, and used in cooking. Red rags seaweed looks similar to dulse, but it is not good to eat.

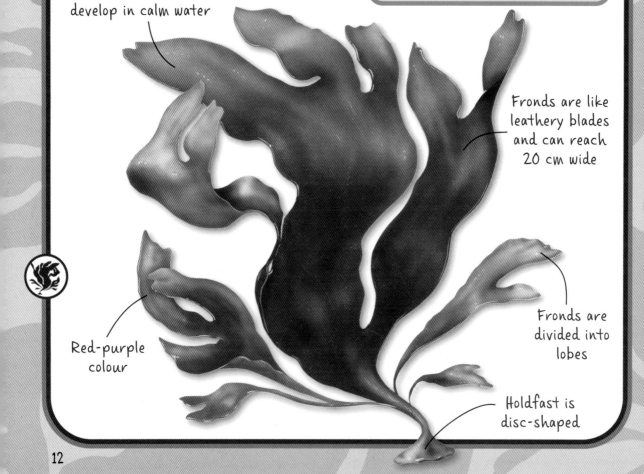

Wide, round lobes develop in calm water

Fronds are like leathery blades and can reach 20 cm wide

Red-purple colour

Fronds are divided into lobes

Holdfast is disc-shaped

KNOTTED WRACK

Often found on rocky shores, knotted wrack is recognisable by the two types of swelling along its slender fronds. The large oval swellings are gas bladders, and are full of air. They help the fronds to float and reach sunlight. The smaller swellings are paler in colour and help the alga reproduce. Knotted wrack rarely grows on shores exposed to big waves and strong winds.

SCALE

Knotted wrack is often covered with tufts of red seaweed called *Polysiphonia*. As *Polysiphonia* grows, it damages the wrack.

FACT FILE

Scientific name
Ascophyllum nodosum

Type Brown algae

Size 30–200 cm

Habitat Middle and upper shore, in rocky places

Other name Egg wrack

Thin, olive-green fronds

Small, yellow-green swellings

Large, oval gas bladder

Tufts of red seaweed

Stipe (stalk) is rounded near the holdfast, but flat further up

Main stems branch into two

OARWEED

This tough seaweed survives well in coastal areas where there are strong waves and wind. Oarweed does not have roots, but is attached to the seabed or to rocks by a secure holdfast. It has thick, glossy fronds and a round stipe (stalk) that can bend without snapping. These algae provide a seashore habitat where small animals can live and shelter.

SCALE

Oarweeds belong to a family of seaweeds called kelps. Underwater forests of kelp make great places for sea creatures to shelter.

FACT FILE

Scientific name
Laminaria digitata

Type Brown algae

Size Up to 200 cm

Habitat Rocks on the lower shore and water up to 6 m deep

Other name Tangleweed

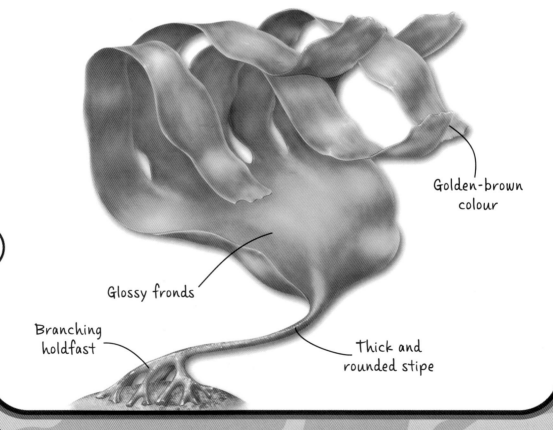

Golden-brown colour

Glossy fronds

Branching holdfast

Thick and rounded stipe

SEA LETTUCE

The appearance of its light green, delicate-looking fronds gives sea lettuce its common name. It grows attached to rocks and pebbles at the top of the shore. Sea lettuce can also survive at river mouths and in shallow salty waters inland. It is sometimes collected for use as a food, and is used in soups.

SCALE

Each plant is either male or female – the edges (margins) of a male plant's fronds are light in colour, but a female has dark margins.

FACT FILE

Scientific name *Ulva lactuca*

Type Green algae

Size 15–40 cm

Habitat Rocky shores, estuaries, rock pools

Other name None

Larger fronds grow in sheltered water

Light can pass through very thin fronds

Margins may be white or dark green

Bright-green colour

Small holdfast

BEADLET ANEMONE

Anemones are related to coral polyps, the tiny animals that build coral reefs. They have soft bodies, but protect themselves from predators with stinging tentacles. These are also used to kill and catch prey as it drifts past. When underwater the tentacles are extended, but they withdraw quickly if disturbed, or when the tide goes out.

SCALE

The best place to find an anemone is in a rock pool, along with other animals such as periwinkles, limpets and small shanny fish.

FACT FILE

Scientific name *Actinia equina*
Type Cnidarian
Size Height up to 7 cm
Habitat Rock pools, rocky shores to depths of 20 m
Other name Red sea anemone

Open with tentacles extended

Tentacles in rows around mouth

Closed with tentacles withdrawn

Body is called the column

Ring of blue dots at top of column

Attached to rock by strong sucker on base

Colour may be red, brown, orange or green

BEWARE! DON'T TOUCH!

BRITTLESTAR

These unusual animals often live in large groups and gather under rocks and in seaweed. If you look under large stones or in cracks and crevices at the very lowest tide, you may be able to find a brittlestar hiding from its predators. Brittlestars are very delicate and should not be touched as they are covered in spines and easily damaged.

SCALE

Offshore, up to 2000 brittlestars can live in one square metre. These strange-looking creatures can be found washed ashore after storms.

FACT FILE

Scientific name
Ophiothrix fragilis

Type Echinoderm

Size 15–22 cm wide

Habitat Lower shore and to depths of 150 m

Other name Common brittlestar

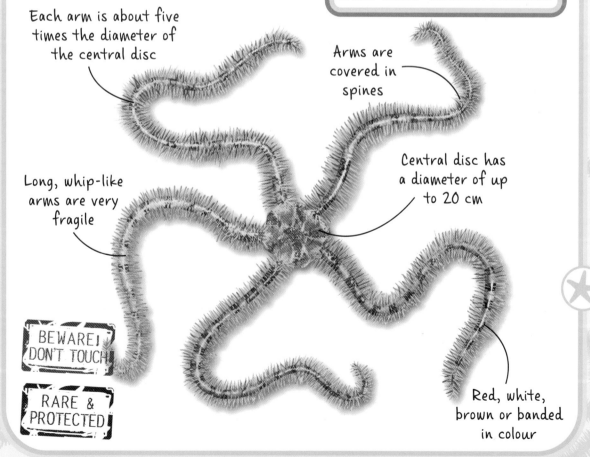

Each arm is about five times the diameter of the central disc

Arms are covered in spines

Long, whip-like arms are very fragile

Central disc has a diameter of up to 20 cm

BEWARE! DON'T TOUCH

RARE & PROTECTED

Red, white, brown or banded in colour

EDIBLE SEA URCHIN

Covered in sharp spines, urchins can cause painful injuries if touched. They graze on seaweed and small marine creatures as they travel across the sea floor, using their powerful mouthparts to grind up food. The shell-like tests (external skeletons) of dead urchins are sometimes washed ashore.

SCALE

A sea urchin's test is made of calcium carbonate, a mineral which is also found in chalk, toothpaste and eggshells.

FACT FILE

Scientific name
Echinus esculentus

Type Echinoderm

Size Up to 10 cm wide

Habitat Lower shore, rock pools, and to depths of 50 m

Other name None

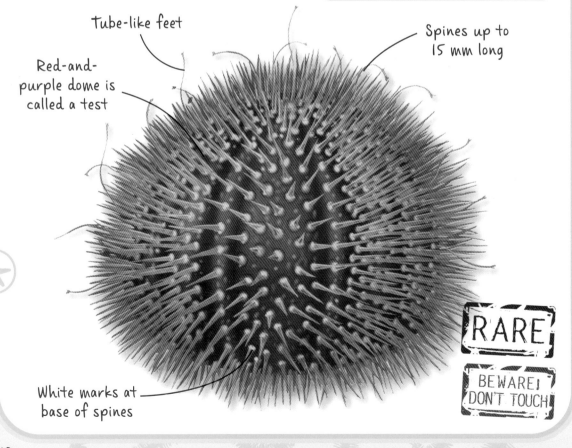

Tube-like feet

Red-and-purple dome is called a test

Spines up to 15 mm long

White marks at base of spines

RARE

BEWARE! DON'T TOUCH

GREEN SEA URCHIN

The tough test, or outer 'shell', of a green sea urchin helps it to withstand strong waves on rocky shores. Short, stubby spines cover the urchins, giving them added protection. The colour of a green sea urchin may provide it with camouflage among seaweed. They often lurk beneath rocks and boulders, hidden from view.

SCALE

These spiky creatures are a relative of the edible sea urchin. They have green spines with violet tips and are found on rocky shores.

FACT FILE

Scientific name
Psammechinus miliaris

Type Echinoderm

Size Up to 5.5 cm wide

Habitat Sand, gravel and rocky shores

Other name Shore urchin

Short, strong spines

Spines are tipped with purple

The test is slightly flattened

BEWARE! DON'T TOUCH

STARFISH

These well-known, widespread creatures can be found on sand, gravel and rocky coasts at low tide, as well as in rock pools. They are commonly found near mussels and barnacles, which they hunt for food. Starfish use their sense of smell to find prey, and eat molluscs by ripping open their shells using the suckers on the undersides of their arms. They can live for up to ten years, and often gather in large groups.

SCALE

Sometimes, big tides wash starfish onto a beach. Once stranded, they are unlikely to make it back to the water, and they die.

FACT FILE

Scientific name *Asterias rubens*

Type Echinoderm

Size Average 15 cm, can grow up to 50 cm

Habitat Lower shore to depths of 200 m

Other name Common starfish

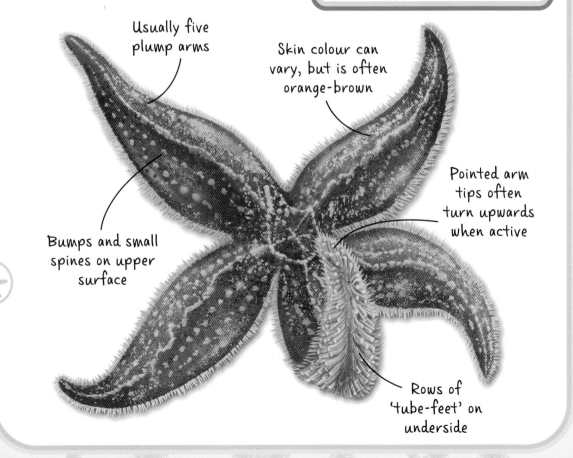

Usually five plump arms

Skin colour can vary, but is often orange-brown

Pointed arm tips often turn upwards when active

Bumps and small spines on upper surface

Rows of 'tube-feet' on underside

COMMON COCKLE

It is unusual to find a live cockle on the shore, but their shells are easy to spot. The living animal inhabits two shells that are tightly joined together when exposed to the air, such as at low tide. Underwater, the shells open so the animal can take in tiny particles of food from the water. Most cockles live for about three years. They are preyed upon by seabirds such as oystercatchers.

SCALE

FACT FILE

Scientific name
Cerastoderma edule

Type Bivalve

Size Up to 5 cm across

Habitat Lower shore in muddy or sandy places, estuaries

Other name Edible cockle

Empty cockle shells are often washed up onto beaches. Their size varies according to their age.

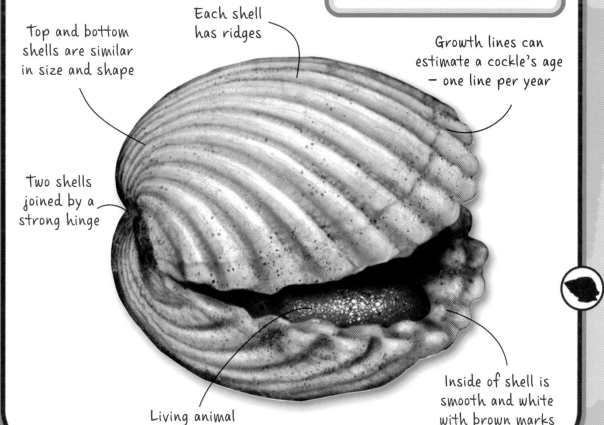

Top and bottom shells are similar in size and shape

Each shell has ridges

Growth lines can estimate a cockle's age – one line per year

Two shells joined by a strong hinge

Living animal

Inside of shell is smooth and white with brown marks

COMMON LIMPET

Limpets belong to the same family as garden slugs and snails. They are found on rocky shores, where they stick firmly to rocks and can leave marks where they have rubbed the surface away. Limpets are protected by their cone-shaped shells and can withstand large waves. Those that live on the upper shore usually have taller shells than those that live on the lower shore.

SCALE

FACT FILE

Scientific name *Patella vulgata*

Type Gastropod

Size Shell 5–7 cm across

Habitat Rocks on middle and upper shore, estuaries

Other name None

Limpets are grazers and move along rocks to feed on algae. As they graze, they may leave paths in the sand.

Shell is cone-shaped

Grey, white or yellowish in colour

Ridges come from the central point

Growth lines

Limpets move around using their foot

COMMON MUSSEL

Like cockles, mussels are bivalves – the animal lives inside two shells that are joined together. They attach themselves to rocky surfaces and open their shells when underwater to feed. Mussels are often found living together in large numbers – these places are called mussel beds. They are preyed upon by seabirds, dog whelks, starfish and sea urchins. Humans also eat mussels.

SCALE

At low tide, mussel beds are exposed to the air. When the tide comes in, the mussels will open their shells again to feed.

FACT FILE

Scientific name *Mytilus edulis*

Type Bivalve

Size Shell up to 10 cm long

Habitat Rocky shores and beds, estuaries

Other name Edible mussel

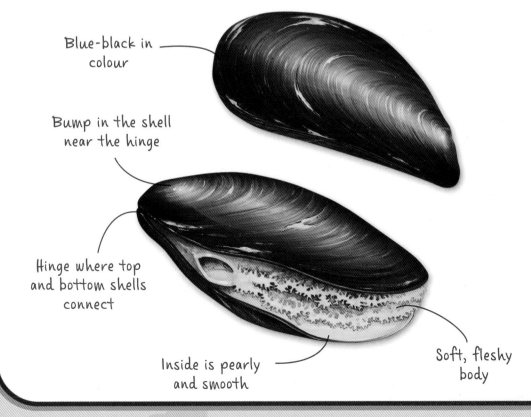

Blue-black in colour

Bump in the shell near the hinge

Hinge where top and bottom shells connect

Inside is pearly and smooth

Soft, fleshy body

COMMON PERIWINKLE

These molluscs live on rocky shores and **can withstand large waves.** They can survive out of water for long periods because they have a flap that covers the opening to their shells. Young periwinkles are dark brown, but become paler with age. These molluscs feed on small particles of food in the sea and seaweed, especially sea lettuce.

SCALE

Periwinkles often live together in large groups. They move along rocks, scraping off seaweed and feeding on it.

FACT FILE

Scientific name
Littorina littorea

Type Gastropod

Size Height of shell 2–3 cm

Habitat Rocky shores, on stones, in seaweed, estuaries

Other name Edible periwinkle

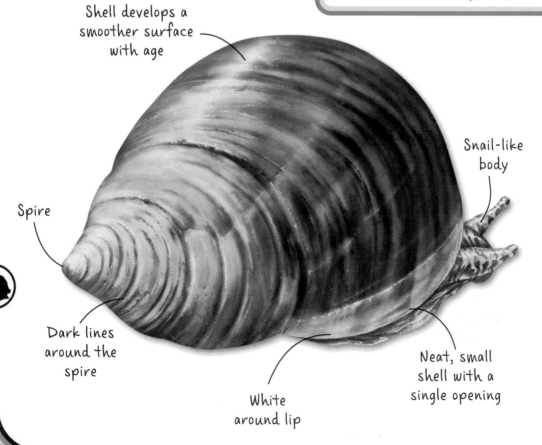

Shell develops a smoother surface with age

Snail-like body

Spire

Dark lines around the spire

White around lip

Neat, small shell with a single opening

DOG WHELK

These small predators are related to garden snails, but unlike their cousins they do not feed on grass. Dog whelks hunt small animals such as barnacles and mussels. They are even able to bore through the shell of another animal to reach the soft flesh inside. Empty whelk shells are often washed up on the shore.

SCALE

Dog whelks lay groups of eggs on rocks during spring. These molluscs can live for up to seven years.

FACT FILE

Scientific name *Nucella lapillus*
Type Gastropod
Size Shell up to 3 cm long
Habitat Rocky shores, especially middle shore
Other name Atlantic dog winkle

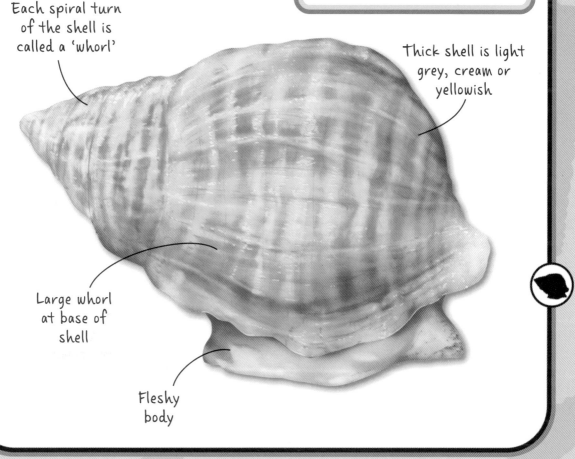

Each spiral turn of the shell is called a 'whorl'

Thick shell is light grey, cream or yellowish

Large whorl at base of shell

Fleshy body

PAINTED TOPSHELL

Topshells usually have coloured or patterned shells. They often have streaks or blotches of colour, and some shells are mostly white. The inside of the shell is pearly and smooth and the opening is protected by a flap, so the animal can survive when the tide goes out. Painted topshells are most commonly found among the holdfasts of seaweeds, where they graze.

SCALE

Painted topshells look bright and shiny because the animal uses its foot to wipe over the shell surface and clean it.

FACT FILE

Scientific name
Calliostoma zizyphinum

Type Gastropod

Size Shell height up to 3 cm

Habitat Rocky shores, especially low shore and among seaweed

Other name None

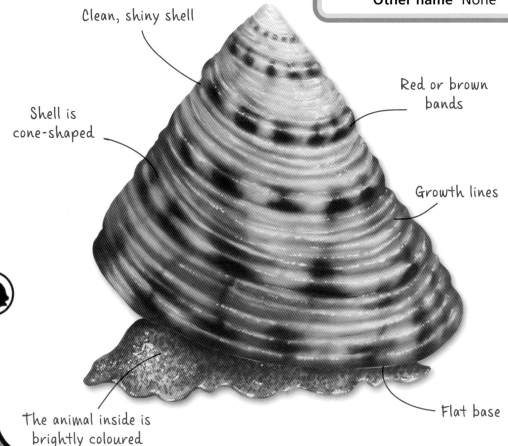

Clean, shiny shell

Red or brown bands

Shell is cone-shaped

Growth lines

The animal inside is brightly coloured

Flat base

RAZOR CLAM

Long, slender shells from razor clams often litter sandy shores, especially after a storm. Usually single shells are washed up, but sometimes two shells can be found, still attached at the hinge-point. There is rarely any sign of the mollusc animal that once lived inside the shells and burrowed deep into the sand. Razor clams feed on tiny animals and plants that live in seawater.

SCALE

Razor clams can only breed when they have reached three years of age, but can live for about ten years.

FACT FILE

Scientific name *Ensis ensis*
Type Bivalve
Size Shell is up to 12.5 cm long
Habitat Sandy shores
Other name Razor shell

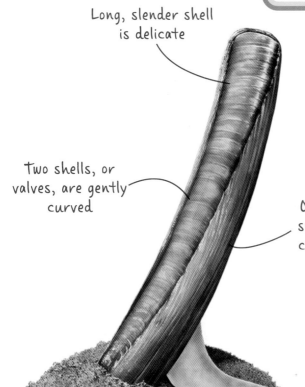

Long, slender shell is delicate

Two shells, or valves, are gently curved

Outside of shell is smooth and white-cream with darker markings

Muscular foot

GLASSWORT

Plants that live near the sea often have salty water around their roots. Only some salt-loving plants, such as glasswort, can cope with these conditions. They often have tiny leaves that grow close to thick, fleshy stems – this helps them store fresh water. Glasswort plants look like small cacti and can be found growing in estuaries and other salty places.

SCALE

In autumn many types of glasswort change colour. Some turn red, others turn purple-pink, orange-red or yellowish.

FACT FILE

Scientific name
Salicornia europaea

Type Salt-loving family

Size Up to 30 cm

Habitat Mud flats, estuaries and saltmarshes

Other name Marsh samphire

Tiny flowers are present from August to September

Plump segments are full of water

Tiny, scale-like leaves

Spikes grow upwards

Bright-green stems in spring and summer

MARRAM GRASS

You can find marram grass growing on sand dunes all over the world. Its thick, green clumps of spiky shoots and leaves help build up the dunes by binding the sand and preventing it from blowing away in the wind. These plants can survive in dry, sandy habitats because their leaves are coated in a wax-like substance that reduces water loss.

SCALE

Areas with marram grass not only support sand dunes — they provide shelter and homes for many insects, animals and plants.

FACT FILE

Scientific name
Ammophila arenaria
Type Grass family
Size Up to 120 cm
Habitat Sand dunes
Other name Beach grass

Leaves are pointed and sharp

Slender, dull-coloured flower spikes from May to August

Leaves have a waxy coating

Long slender leaves and shoots grow in a thick clump

SCARLET PIMPERNEL

This delicate plant is common in gardens, farmland and parks, but it also grows on sand dunes and stony places in coastal areas. It has small red flowers that only open when it is sunny. Scarlet pimpernels do not grow tall, but creep over the ground, covering it in green stems and leaves. Insects are attracted to the flowers in spring and summer.

SCALE

Bog pimpernels are a similar species. They have small pink flowers and grow on boggy ground, dunes and moorland.

FACT FILE

Scientific name
Anagallis arvensis

Type Primrose family

Size Up to 20 cm

Habitat Farms, grassland, sand dunes

Other names Red chickweed

Bright scarlet flowers from May to September

Egg-shaped leaves

Creeping stems

Black dots on undersides of leaves

SEA KALE

Most often found on shingle beaches, sea kale can also survive in the dry, sandy parts of the upper shore. Its thick leaves are able to store water and have a waxy coating on their surface to stop too much water evaporating. Sea kale rarely flowers before reaching five years of age. It used to be steamed and eaten, but is now rare and should never be picked.

SCALE

After a sea kale has flowered, the seed pods slowly ripen. They dry out and up to 10,000 seeds are released.

FACT FILE

Scientific name
Crambe maritima

Type Cabbage family

Size Up to 100 cm across

Habitat Upper sandy or shingle shores, pebbly beaches, cliffs

Other name Colewort

Large, thick leaves are green or purple

Waxy coating on the leaves

Clusters of white flowers from June to August

RARE & PROTECTED

Plant grows in a dome shape

SEA PEA

Pretty sea pea plants bring colour to dry areas of shingle beaches. Their delicate leaves and tendrils spread out in clumps up to two metres wide. Sea peas rarely flower before their third summer. The pea-like seeds are carried by seawater to new areas, and can survive for up to five years before they start to grow into new plants.

SCALE

Long-tongued bees are attracted to the flowers, and pollinate them. Pigeons and doves eat the pea-sized seeds.

FACT FILE

Scientific name
Lathyrus japonicus

Type Pea family

Size Up to 20 cm

Habitat Upper shore, dry shingle, sandy banks

Other name Beach pea

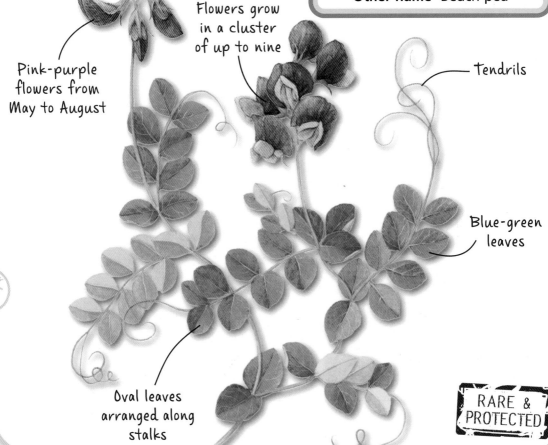

Pink-purple flowers from May to August

Flowers grow in a cluster of up to nine

Tendrils

Blue-green leaves

Oval leaves arranged along stalks

RARE & PROTECTED

SILVERWEED

This creeping plant grows in grassy areas and on bare ground, including sandy and shingle shores. It grows best in the damp, but can survive periods of dry weather. The leaves are feathery and divided into many pairs of leaflets, which are covered in fine hairs. Long, creeping stems, called stolons, trail along the ground between the leaves and flowers.

SCALE

On cloudy days and at night, the leaves of a silverweed plant may be closed. On sunny days they open up.

FACT FILE

Scientific name
Potentilla anserina

Type Rose family

Size 5–20 cm

Habitat Cliffs, upper shingle, sandy shores

Other name Cinquefoil

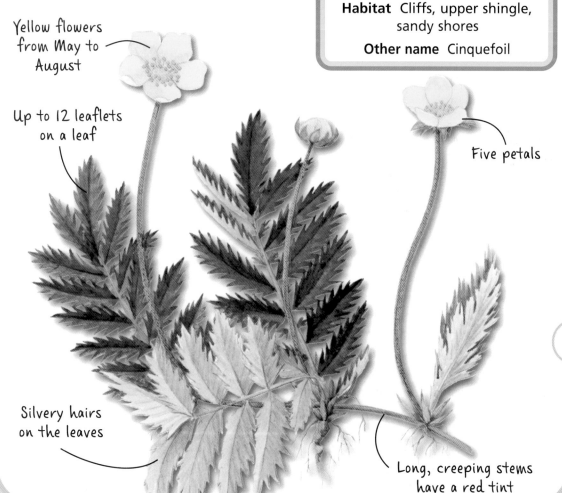

Yellow flowers from May to August

Up to 12 leaflets on a leaf

Five petals

Silvery hairs on the leaves

Long, creeping stems have a red tint

THRIFT

Thrift can survive on upper shores and cliffs because it likes dry habitats. Its candyfloss-pink flowerheads grow above a dense mat of leaves from April to October. This pretty plant forms a round, cushion-like clump and the leaves remain once the flowers have died back. As the flowerheads age they become paler in colour, dry and papery.

SCALE

Most thrift flowers are pink, but they may also be white or red. They thrive on cliffs and are also popular garden plants.

FACT FILE

Scientific name
Armeria maritima
Type Thrift family
Size Up to 20 cm
Habitat Rocky places, cliffs
Other names Sea pink

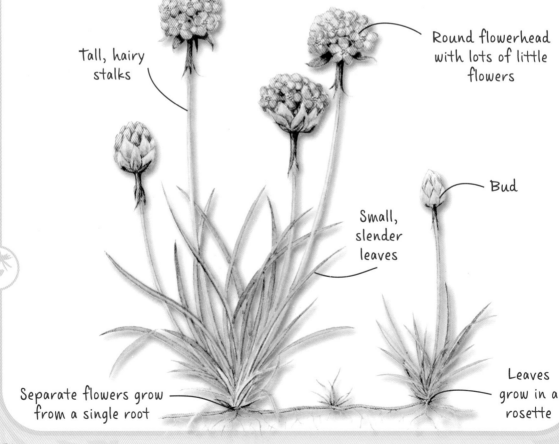

Tall, hairy stalks

Round flowerhead with lots of little flowers

Bud

Small, slender leaves

Separate flowers grow from a single root

Leaves grow in a rosette

HERMIT CRAB

These common coastal creatures are more closely related to lobsters than crabs. Their skins are quite soft, so they get extra protection by setting up home in empty shells. Their bodies are twisted to fit comfortably inside. Occasionally, they find a bigger, better shell and do a quick swap. These crustaceans forage on the seashore looking for carrion (dead animals) to eat.

SCALE

FACT FILE

Scientific name
Pagurus bernhardus

Type Decapod

Size 2–6 cm long

Habitat Shallow water, rock pools, rocky shores, sandy shores

Other name Soldier crab

Plants and animals may live on a hermit crab's shell. Barnacles and sea anemones are common hitchhikers.

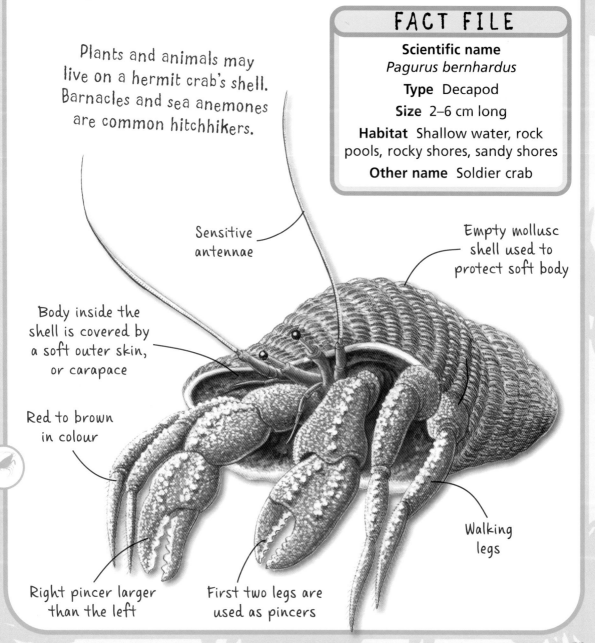

Sensitive antennae

Empty mollusc shell used to protect soft body

Body inside the shell is covered by a soft outer skin, or carapace

Red to brown in colour

Walking legs

Right pincer larger than the left

First two legs are used as pincers

NORTHERN ACORN BARNACLE

It is unusual to see a live barnacle, but it is easy to find their tough, protective shells. Barnacles cover many seashore rocks and can even be found growing on mollusc shells. When the tide is out, the barnacle shell is closed, but once underwater it opens and the tiny animal pokes its feathery limbs out to feed on food particles floating in the seawater.

SCALE

FACT FILE

Scientific name
Semibalanus balanoides

Type Cirriped

Size Up to 15 mm wide

Habitat Middle to upper shore, in rocky places

Other name None

The empty shells of dead barnacles have lost their terminal plates (see below). Living barnacles survive alongside the dead ones.

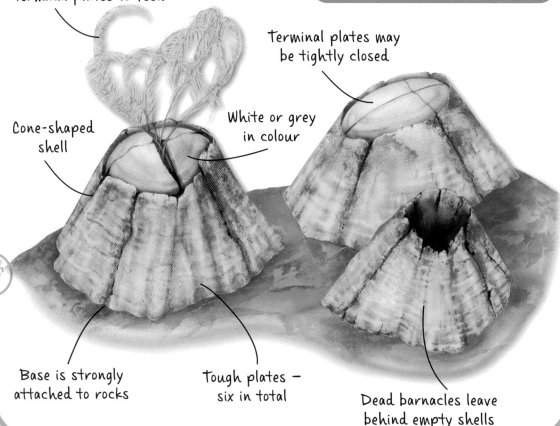

Curved, feathery limbs emerge from between terminal plates to feed

Cone-shaped shell

White or grey in colour

Terminal plates may be tightly closed

Base is strongly attached to rocks

Tough plates — six in total

Dead barnacles leave behind empty shells

36

SAND HOPPER

Also known as beach fleas, these small creatures often gather in large numbers along the strandline. This marks the highest place that the tide reaches on a beach and so seaweed, shells and stones collect here. During the day, sand hoppers mostly stay hidden, buried in the sand – but in the evening they emerge to hop between the seaweed and look for food.

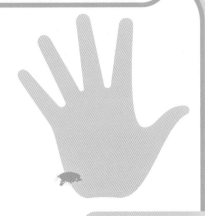

SCALE

FACT FILE

Scientific name
Orchestia gammarellus

Type Amphipod

Size Up to 18 mm long

Habitat On all shores, especially where seaweed is stranded

Other name Beach flea

Large sand hoppers — *Talitrus saltator* — bury themselves in sand, and can dig down to depths of 30 cm.

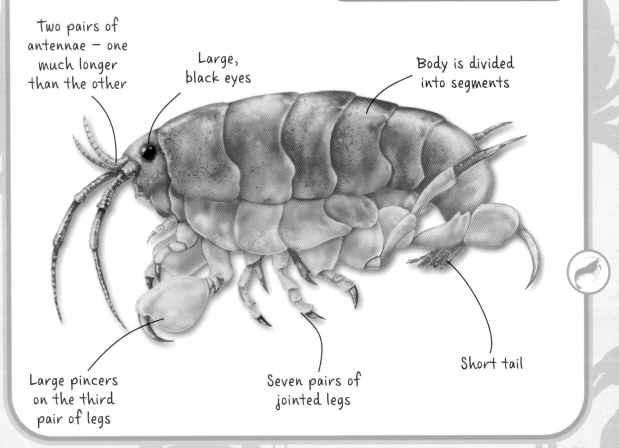

Two pairs of antennae — one much longer than the other

Large, black eyes

Body is divided into segments

Large pincers on the third pair of legs

Seven pairs of jointed legs

Short tail

SHORE CRAB

Crabs have five pairs of legs, although the front pair has powerful pincers. They use their pincers to fight and catch prey. Shore crabs feed on molluscs, worms and other crustaceans. They also eat the remains of dead fish that have been washed ashore. During summer, you are likely to find young crabs as well as older adults on the shore and in rock pools.

SCALE

Crabs frequently fight, and may be left with just one claw after losing the other one in a battle.

FACT FILE

Scientific name
Carcinus maenas

Type Decapod

Size Up to 10 cm wide

Habitat All shores and shallow water, estuaries

Other name European green crab

Pointed hind legs grip onto pebbles

Can be green or brown

Tough outer skin (carapace) is wider than it is long

Second and third pairs of legs are long

Eyes on stalks can move around

Powerful pincers on first pair of legs

SHRIMP

Shrimps can be hard to spot, because they are almost transparent (see-through) and very well camouflaged. These small crustaceans spend most of the day hiding in the sand, emerging at sunset to feed. Shrimps are food for many seabirds that wade through shallow water, probing the sand and mud with their bills.

SCALE

Shrimps walk along the seabed looking for small worms, molluscs and crustaceans to feed on.

FACT FILE

Scientific name
Crangon crangon

Type Decapod

Size 3–5 cm long

Habitat Shallow water, rock pools

Other name Brown shrimp

Very long, slender antennae

Flattened body is divided into segments

Carapace grows into long spines between the eyes

Curved abdomen

Light brown in colour with some flecks

Fan-like tail

VELVET SWIMMING CRAB

Most crabs scuttle along the shore and seabed, hiding beneath rocks or digging into sand. Velvet swimming crabs can also run extremely quickly and they are good swimmers. Their last pair of legs are flattened, like paddles, to help them swim. Velvet swimming crabs are best left alone – they can be aggressive if touched and their strong pincers can give a painful injury.

SCALE

The velvet swimming crab is a grazer and a predator. It hides in seaweed or anemones, looking for prey.

FACT FILE

Scientific name *Necora puber*

Type Decapod

Size Length and width up to 8 cm

Habitat Low shore and shallow water, especially among rocks

Other name Devil crab

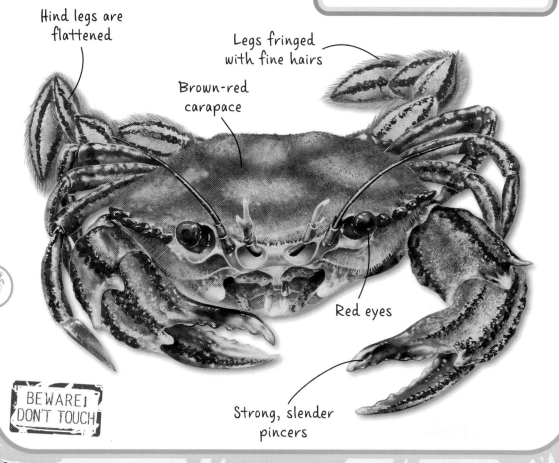

Hind legs are flattened

Legs fringed with fine hairs

Brown-red carapace

Red eyes

Strong, slender pincers

BEWARE! DON'T TOUCH!

CINNABAR MOTH

Eating a diet of toxic ragwort plants as caterpillars gives these moths a foul flavour. The toxins are transferred into the moth's body, and this insect's bold colouring warns predators not to take a bite. Cinnabar caterpillars are just as easy to identify, with thick, black-and-gold bands along the whole length of their bodies. They are most active at night, but can be seen flitting to flowers and feeding during the daytime too.

SCALE

FACT FILE

Scientific name *Tyria jacobaeae*
Type Lepidopteran
Wingspan 3.5–4 cm
Habitat Sand dunes, wastelands and meadows
Other name None

These moths are named after cinnabar, a red mineral that is sometimes used as a pigment to create colours.

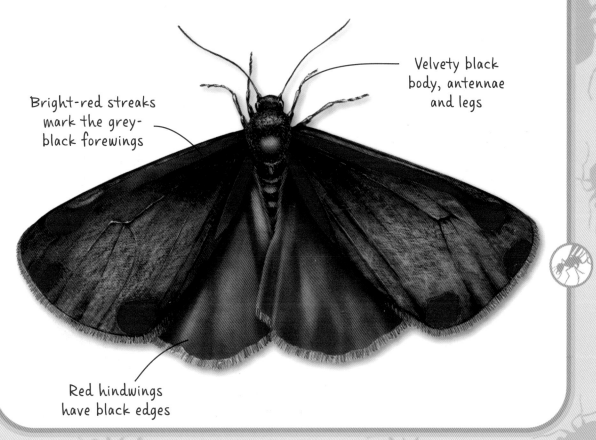

Bright-red streaks mark the grey-black forewings

Velvety black body, antennae and legs

Red hindwings have black edges

COMMON BLUE BUTTERFLY

These pretty blue butterflies are most likely to be spotted between May and September. They feed on nectar from large, flat-headed flowers and can be seen in coastal areas, especially around sand dunes. The larvae are green with yellow stripes along their sides and a dark line down their backs. They produce a substance from their skin that attracts ants, and in turn, the ants protect the larvae from predators.

SCALE

Common blues are most active in the sunshine, especially males. They fly around looking for flowers and females.

FACT FILE

Scientific name
Polyommatus icarus

Type Lepidopteran

Wingspan 3–4 cm long

Habitat Dunes, sandy shores, cliffs, grasslands and gardens

Other name None

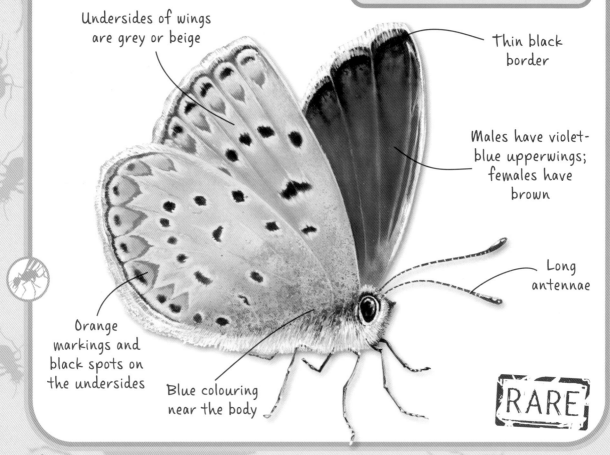

Undersides of wings are grey or beige

Thin black border

Males have violet-blue upperwings; females have brown

Long antennae

Orange markings and black spots on the undersides

Blue colouring near the body

RARE

GRAYLING BUTTERFLY

The grayling is quite a large butterfly so it is easy to spot when in flight. Once it settles on sand, mud or rocks however, it becomes almost invisible. These insects prefer sunny, dry spots and the adults are active from June to the middle of September. Grayling caterpillars feed on grasses and are brown and cream in colour.

SCALE

Grayling caterpillars are hard to find, as they hide on blades of grass and mostly feed at night.

FACT FILE

Scientific name
Hipparchia semele

Type Lepidopteran

Wingspan Up to 6 cm

Habitat Dunes, coastal paths, cliffs and hedges

Other name None

Dark eye spots on forewings

Orange parts may be hidden when settled

Long antennae

Whitish band

Only four legs are visible as the front two are very small

Mottled brown underside

Sea holly

RARE

GREEN TIGER BEETLE

These brightly coloured beetles are common in the British Isles. They have a beautiful green metallic sheen and are easy to spot, especially on sunny summer days. Green tiger beetles have long legs and can run very fast when they chase other insects to eat. These insects can also fly, and make a loud buzzing sound when in the air.

SCALE

When a green tiger beetle is disturbed it launches into short, buzzing flights. These beetles fly unusually fast.

FACT FILE

Scientific name
Cicindela campestris
Type Coleopteran
Size Up to 15 mm long
Habitat Sand dunes, sandy shores, cliffs
Other name Common green tiger beetle

Shiny, metallic green colour

Yellow spots on wing cases

Three pairs of jointed legs

Bulging eyes

Long, hooked antennae

RED-BANDED SAND WASP

With long black bodies and red bands, these stinging insects are easy to spot. Red-banded sand wasps belong to the same family as bees and wasps. They use their stings to stun caterpillars, which are then dragged to the wasps' nests. The wasps lay their eggs inside the caterpillars' bodies. When the eggs hatch, the wasp larvae feed on the live caterpillars.

SCALE

The wasp uses its jaws to hold a caterpillar while stinging it. The small stinger is on the tip of the abdomen.

FACT FILE

Scientific name
Ammophila sabulosa

Type Hymenopteran

Size Up to 25 mm long

Habitat Sand dunes, sandy upper shores

Other name Sand digger wasp

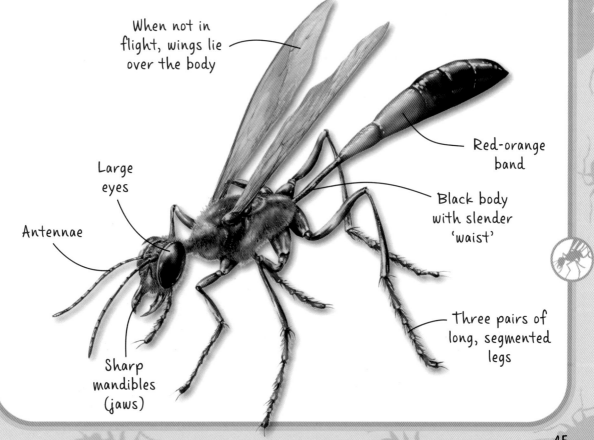

When not in flight, wings lie over the body

Large eyes

Antennae

Sharp mandibles (jaws)

Red-orange band

Black body with slender 'waist'

Three pairs of long, segmented legs

AVOCET

These beautiful wading birds are found in coastal habitats, especially in eastern England. They have distinctive black-and-white plumage, long legs and unusually long bills, which they use to sweep through mud, searching for insects, shelled animals and worms to eat. Avocets became extinct in Britain in the 19th century, but they were successfully reintroduced to England in the 1940s.

SCALE

FACT FILE

Scientific name
Recurvirostra avosetta

Type Wader

Wingspan 67–77 cm

Habitat Estuaries, coastal lagoons

Other name None

Avocets build their nests in dry areas, but bring their chicks to muddy flats to feed.

Black cap and hind neck

White patches on wings

Black bars on wings

Long, black bill curves upwards

Long, grey legs

RARE

COMMON TERN

Sometimes called sea swallows because of the graceful way they fly, common terns swoop into the sea to catch fish. Elegant but aggressive, this bird is seen across Britain in the summer. It nests in noisy colonies and flies, often out at sea, in search of food. When they spot fish below them, terns plunge-dive into the water in pursuit of their prey.

SCALE

Both parents look after their eggs, but common tern chicks are mostly cared for, and fed, by their fathers.

FACT FILE

Scientific name *Sterna hirundo*

Type Tern

Wingspan 82–95 cm

Habitat Shingle beaches, estuaries, cliffs, inland gravel pits and reservoirs

Other name Tern

Pale underwing with dark band at back edge

Grey back to upperwing

Black cap

Bright-red bill with a black tip

Long, forked tail

Orange feet

CORMORANT

These unusual-looking water birds have angular bodies and dark feathers. They are superb swimmers and live all around Britain's coasts. When a cormorant catches a fish, it shakes it before swallowing it whole. Cormorants have large, webbed feet used for swimming and for incubating their eggs, which they hold between the tops of their feet and their warm bodies.

SCALE

It takes a great deal of muscle power and energy for a cormorant to lift its body out of the sea.

FACT FILE

Scientific name
Phalacrocorax carbo

Type Cormorant

Wingspan 130–160 cm

Habitat Rocky shores, estuaries, some inland lakes and reservoirs

Other name Sea raven

Glossy back

White cheeks and chin

Long, yellow bill with small hook at tip

Long, broad tail

White patch in summer

CURLEW

Some curlews live in Britain all year, in coastal areas and other water habitats. Others spend the winter here, and fly north when spring arrives. These waders are known for their beautiful spring song, which has been described as eerie or ghost-like. Curlews often gather in large numbers to feed, particularly at mud flats on estuaries.

SCALE

Curlews are the largest of all wading birds in Europe. They are common around estuaries and coasts in January and February.

FACT FILE

Scientific name
Numenius arquata

Type Wader

Wingspan 80–100 cm

Habitat Estuaries, inland grasslands and uplands

Other name Eurasian curlew

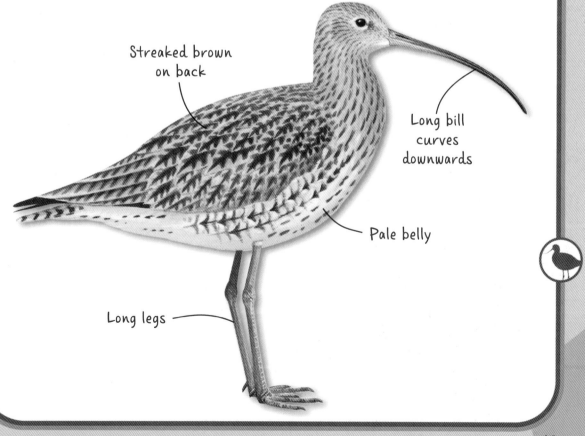

Streaked brown on back

Long bill curves downwards

Pale belly

Long legs

HERRING GULL

These birds are well known to holiday makers at seaside towns and beaches. Herring gulls have little fear of humans and will approach them for food. They have other ways of feeding though, such as trampling on mud to make worms come to the surface. In recent years, the number of herring gulls in Britain has dramatically fallen. Scientists are not sure why these birds are struggling to survive in coastal areas.

SCALE

Herring gulls have bright-yellow bills and an obvious red spot on the lower bill. They fly by soaring and gliding on the wind.

FACT FILE

Scientific name *Larus argentatus*
Type Gull
Wingspan 130–160 cm
Habitat Cliffs, islands, mudflats, beaches especially in northern and eastern areas
Other name European herring gull

Pure-white head

Yellow eyes

Pale grey back

Yellow bill with red spot

Black wing tips with white spots

Pale pink legs

KNOT

Large flocks of knots gather around river mouths and estuaries during the winter months, especially in eastern areas. They spend spring and summer in the Arctic, where they breed, and at this time their plumage becomes much darker. Knots feed on small animals such as molluscs, crustaceans and worms, which they find in the muddy shores and coastal mudflats.

SCALE

FACT FILE

Scientific name *Calidris canutus*
Type Wader
Wingspan 47–54 cm
Habitat Estuaries, muddy beaches
Other name Red knot

Knots are a type of coastal bird that look similar to dunlins. Dunlins have longer bills and darker markings.

Pale stripe above eye

Straight, long bill

Feathers are mottled grey, white and light brown

Stocky body

Belly is paler than the back

Short legs

OYSTERCATCHER

Bright, bold and noisy, oystercatchers are easy to identify. These birds live in coastal regions throughout the year and often form enormous flocks. They walk along seashores or mudflats with their heads down, searching for food. Oystercatchers use their strong bills to break open shellfish such as cockles and mussels. Despite their name, they do not appear to eat oysters.

SCALE

FACT FILE

Scientific name
Haematopus ostralegus

Type Wader

Wingspan 80–85 cm

Habitat Sandy, muddy and rocky beaches

Other name Pied oystercatcher

Limpets may be able to stick tightly to rocks, but oystercatchers can use their strong bills to prise them off.

Red eye

Long, bright-orange bill

Black-and-white plumage

Large, bulky body

Short, pale pink legs

REDSHANK

These wading birds breed throughout the British Isles, especially in areas near water. When the breeding season is over, redshanks move towards the coast and estuaries. They wade through shallow water to search for molluscs, worms, crustaceans and insects to eat. Redshanks gather in large flocks, often perching on posts or breakwaters, and make loud alarm calls when disturbed.

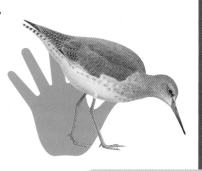

SCALE

FACT FILE

Scientific name *Tringa tetanus*

Type Wader

Wingspan 45–50 cm

Habitat Marshes, coastal mudflats, estuaries, uplands

Other name Common redshank

Many redshanks in southwest England are winter visitors, flying in from Iceland.

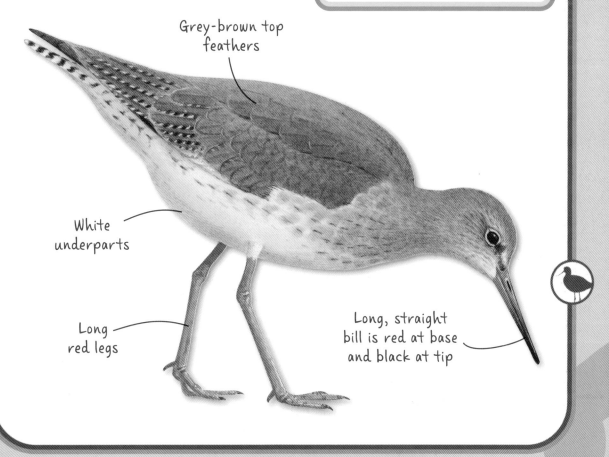

Grey-brown top feathers

White underparts

Long red legs

Long, straight bill is red at base and black at tip

RINGED PLOVER

Short and stocky, ringed plovers are small wading birds that usually gather in large flocks, especially at high tide. They have obvious black markings next to their white feathers. This bold pattern helps the birds to blend in against shingle and pebbles on the beach.

SCALE

Found all year round, these plump little birds eat insects, crustaceans and worms along the shore.

FACT FILE

Scientific name
Charadrius hiaticula

Type Wader

Wingspan 48–58 cm

Habitat Sandy beaches, shingle shores and inland gravel pits

Other name None

White stripe just above eye

Sandy-coloured feathers on back

Bill is short with orange-and-black bands

Dark band across breast

Camouflaged eggs

Orange legs

SHELDUCK

Although some shelducks live inland, **most live in coastal habitats and can be seen all year round.** These large ducks have a call similar to that of some geese. Shelducks wade through shallow water, sweeping their bills from side to side as they hunt for animals such as crustaceans to eat. They also graze on seaweed.

SCALE

Shelducks usually lay their nests on the ground. Adults birds often look after chicks that are not their own.

FACT FILE

Scientific name
Tadorna tadorna

Type Wildfowl

Wingspan 110–130 cm

Habitat Sandy and muddy shores, estuaries

Other names Sheldrake

Dark green-black head

Bright-red bill with knob above nostrils

Mostly white plumage

Rusty-coloured band on chest

Green flash

Pink legs

GLOSSARY

Algae A group of simple, plant-like organisms including seaweeds.

Amphipod A type of small crustacean that looks like a tiny shrimp.

Bivalve A group of molluscs that have two shells joined by a hinge.

Camouflage The way that an animal's colour, markings or shape enable it to blend in with its surroundings.

Carapace The hard body casing that protects the body of a crustacean.

Cirriped A type of crustacean with external body parts that catch food, such as barnacles.

Cnidarian The main group of soft-bodied animals, such as jellyfish.

Coleopteran A type of beetle that has forewings modified into hard wing-cases.

Crustacean A group of animals that usually have a hard body casing and jointed limbs, such as crabs.

Decapod The main group of ten-legged crustaceans, such as lobsters.

Echinoderm The main group of 'spiny-skinned' marine animals, such as sea urchins and starfish.

Estuary The mouth of a river where it widens and flows into the sea.

Frond The broad, flat leaves of water plants, such as seaweed.

Gastropod A group of animals including slugs and snails, which move using a single muscular 'foot'.

Habitat The place where an animal or plant lives.

Holdfast The roots that anchor plants such as seaweed to surfaces.

Hymenopteran A group of insects including bees, wasps and ants that usually have a sting.

Lepidopteran A group of insects with two pairs of large wings covered with scales that form colours and patterns, such as butterflies.

Mollusc A group of soft-bodied animals without backbones. Some types have a hard outer shell.

Predator An animal that hunts and eats other animals.

Prey An animal that is hunted and eaten by other animals.

Stalk The long, narrow part of a plant that supports the leaves, flowers and fruit, and carries water and nutrients up them.

Stem The thin part of a plant from which the leaves and flowers grow.

Stipe The strong and flexible stem-like structure of seaweed.

Stolons Shoots of a plant that grow horizontally above or just below the ground.

Tendril A thin, thread-like part of a climbing plant that wraps itself around things.

Venom A harmful substance made by an animal's body, which can be injected into another creature.